101 TIPS FOR FIDDLE

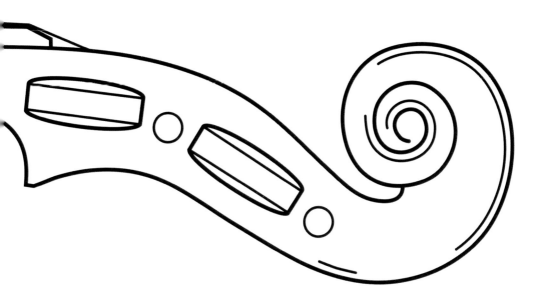

BY
PHILIP JOHN BERTHOUD

CONTENTS

The left-hand fingers* are numbered:

Index finger – 1st finger
Middle finger – 2nd finger
Ring finger – 3rd finger
Little finger – 4th finger

The fiddle strings are numbered 1st to 4th. The 1st string is the thinnest and the 4th is the thickest.

It has been assumed that the reader is right-handed. Therefore the fingering hand is referred to as the left hand, the bowing hand as the right hand. If you are left-handed, please adjust accordingly.

BOWING

1

Know your bow. Here's a picture with the different parts labelled:

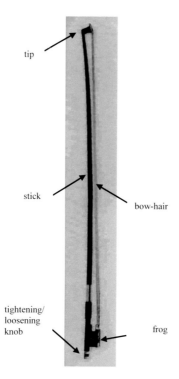

tip

stick

bow-hair

tightening/
loosening
knob

frog

2

The bow should be held just tightly enough to stop it falling from your hand. Gripping tightly will hamper freedom of movement and also make your playing sound heavy and laboured, not to mention the possibility of aches and pains in the wrist and/or hand.

3

To emphasise notes, it is not always necessary to press the bow harder onto the string. A very effective way is simply to speed up the movement of the bow. This helps to retain the lightness that is so vital to good traditional playing.

picture a

The bow may be held right next to the frog (picture a) or further up the stick (picture b). The former grip is used by all classical and many other types of player. The latter is used by many traditional players and baroque musicians.

picture b

5

When bowing a note, you should be guiding the bow on its course over the string. Don't force it. The act of drawing the bow over the string should be as easy and relaxed as possible.

6

Experiment with using other parts of the bow hair when playing tunes. Try playing a tune you know well just using the four inches or so of bow from the tip end. Do the same from the frog end, and the middle of the bow. To help you keep within these limits, a small sticker or two could be put on the stick of the bow. Practicing like this will improve your overall control of the bow.

When playing a scale try it with slurred bowing as well as separate bowing. For example:

G major scale (1 octave) slurred in pairs

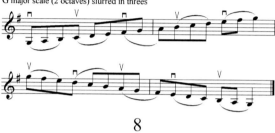

G major scale (2 octaves) slurred in threes

8

If plucking the string, do not do this where the bow comes into contact with the string – do it further up the string, over the fingerboard. Grease on the string from the fingers may interfere with the sound when bowing.

9

For the best tone the bow should make contact with the string in the area midway between the bridge and the end of the fingerboard. For a louder, more strident tone, play nearer the bridge.

10

When playing traditional dance tunes play with separate
bow movements for a stronger, more strident sound.
For a smoother, mellower sound use more slurs.
Compare the two examples below:

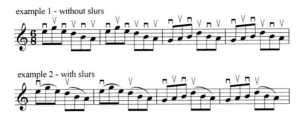

Ideally there would be a mixture of the two, as in the
last two bars of example 2, above.

11

Move the bow across the strings confidently. Bouncing
bows and a scratchy sound are problems that could be
blamed on a cautious approach. The bow is very
unforgiving, and will expose any lack of confidence.
Don't be afraid to use it.

12

To achieve the "light touch", which works so well on
faster tunes, the secret is to use less bow. Using too
much bow can make it very difficult to play up to speed,
and will result in a more laboured, heavy sound.
Experiment with using a small amount of the bow's
length. For example:

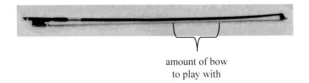

amount of bow
to play with

13

When playing slow tunes, make allowances for the fact
that the bow will change direction more slowly. This
may lead to the common problem of "running out of
bow". Maybe change some bow directions so that it
works better for you.

FINGERING

Ensure the left-hand fingers don't press the strings down too hard, especially when playing louder. Use just the minimum pressure required. To discover this minimum pressure level, do the following-

- Put a left-hand finger down on a note.
- Now release the pressure exerted by that finger, so that it is just resting on the string.
- Start bowing the string. The fact that your finger is just resting on the string will mean that the sound will be rather unpleasant.
- While still bowing, very slowly increase the pressure exerted by the left hand finger until a clear note can be heard. This will be the minimum pressure required.
- Now play that note with long bows, short bows, loudly and softly, all the time remembering to maintain the same pressure with the left hand finger.
- Try this exercise with different fingers.

15

The fiddle is an ideal instrument for executing slides – a staple technique for the traditional fiddler. A slide, as the name implies, involve sliding the finger up or down the string (usually up), gradually altering the pitch of the note.

To play a rising slide, choose a note to slide up to. Put the finger down in a lower (flatter) position than it would do to normally play that note. Play the "out-of-tune" note and slide up to the desired note. Be careful not to "overshoot" beyond the destination note.

The descending slide should be used with more caution. Rather than sliding down to a desired note, this technique is normally used to achieve the effect of "falling away" from the main note.

The most common is the slide that moves up to a destination note. Generally speaking, North American fiddlers use a longer slide than those from Ireland or Scotland. That is they start from a flatter, or lower sounding note.

Devote some time to exercises for the little finger. This finger is normally underused. As a result, it may be less accurate/strong/able to move independently than the other fingers. Try the following exercises, where the little finger notes are shown by the figure 4:

17

Playing speed and fluency can be seriously hampered by gripping the neck of the fiddle too tightly. Aim to hold the neck loosely, in a relaxed way, only using pressure when and where required.

To improve intonation (how in tune your playing is), play a familiar tune in a more difficult key. This involves transposing the tune, i.e. moving all the notes up or down in pitch by the same amount. Melody #1 below starts on D and is then shown starting on E♭. This means moving each note up one semitone higher than the original. Melody #2 is moved up a tone, the first changing from A to B.

melody #1 starting on D

melody #1 starting on E flat

melody #2 starting on A

melody #2 starting on B

Keep unused left-hand fingers hovering just above the finger-board, ready for when they are needed. Don't allow them to stray too far as this will affect your playing speed and fluency.

BAD

GOOD

Look at the three pictures below, all showing the left hand first finger playing B on the A string.

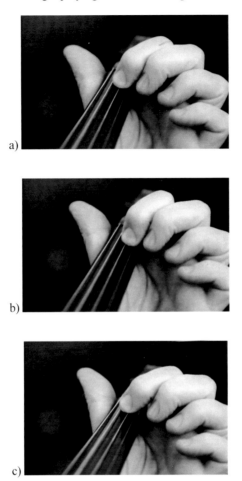

a)

b)

c)

A different part of the finger tip is being used in each picture:

a) In this picture the finger is placed centrally on the string.

b) The next picture shows the finger closer to the E string, although it is still holding down the A string.

c) In the third picture the finger is nearer the D string

See tip 21

To illustrate tip 20 further, look at the music examples below. In all of them, the B note is to be held down for the duration of the two bars.

To play examples 1 and 2 comfortably and quickly, the first finger will need to be clear of the 3rd string, while holding down the B at the same time – see photo b) in tip 20.

For examples 3 and 4, the first finger will need to be clear of the first string, so the position shown in photo c) of the previous tip will be more suitable.

This way of fingering is very useful for quick playing.

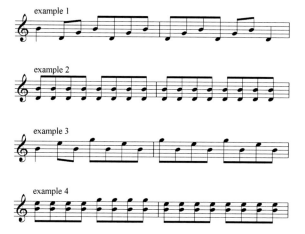

22

Ensure there is a minimum of tension in your body when playing either seated or standing. Common areas to watch out for include:

- **shoulders** – these should not be hunched and, if you use a shoulder rest, this should be adjusted so that you can hold the fiddle comfortably between the shoulder/collar bone and chin. (see photo below)

- **arms** – these should be relaxed and not forced into position.

- **hands** – not gripping too tightly, whether it's the fingerboard or bow.

- **fingers** – avoid unnecessary movement or gripping too hard.

- **jaw** – clenching teeth – not as strange as it sounds, can be a problem if the fiddle is being held too tightly between the chin and collar bone.

23

Every so often, practice in front of a mirror to check that your posture is good and also that the bow is in right place, at right angles to the strings.

24

Make sure your back is straight when playing. This applies when seated or standing. If you play seated, make sure the back doesn't twist round to make room for the bow. Instead, adjust your seating posture. Playing regularly with a twisted back will increase the likelihood of strain. Ask someone to stand behind you to check if your back is straight when playing if this is a problem for you.

25

The right-hand wrist needs to be supple and relaxed.
This is true for all styles of music, when playing loudly
or softly. Any tension in this area will be reflected in
the sound.

26

Rules for classical violinists on how to hold the
instrument do not have to apply for the traditional
fiddler. A more relaxed approach – i.e. holding the
instrument/bow in a way that is comfortable for you
(without impeding playing) – is more appropriate.

27

While foot-tapping is obviously undesirable for
orchestral players, it is to be positively encouraged for
traditional players. Traditional music is not described as
"foot-tapping" for nothing!

28

It is not uncommon for a player's posture to alter when
playing very fast or intensely. This is fine, so long as
the body is still relaxed. Keep a look out for extra
tension when playing in this way.

29

At the start of each practice session, get your fingers warmed up by playing through some scales. If you are not sure what to do, there are many inexpensive scale books available to the fiddle player.

30

Plan your practice sessions. Here is a possible format for a 1 hour practice:

Tune up	
Warm up with scales/exercises	10 mins
Run through tune to practice	5 mins
Play through again, slowly, identifying any problem areas	10 mins
Isolate problem areas, analyse difficulties and ascertain what work needs to be done – change fingering, change bowing etc	15mins
Play through tune again, this time with alterations made	10 mins
Play through some other music that you know well and enjoy.	10 mins

Use this as a guide. Make your own timetable better suited to your own needs/timescale.

31

Practice time is a great opportunity to work on difficult tunes, ironing out problem areas and concentrating on improving technique. However, it is also great to play music you know really well and to enjoy the fact that it sounds good. Practice doesn't always have to be hard work.

When practicing at home, imagine that you are playing in front of a large, highly appreciative audience. It is surprising how much this can do for your confidence.

33

If you are learning a new tune, it can be frustrating if there is one bit that always bugs you because it's difficult. A potentially exciting tune can be spoilt as a result. To help with this, ascertain which group of notes is causing the problem and play them over and over again more slowly – creating a useful exercise from the difficult notes. For example:

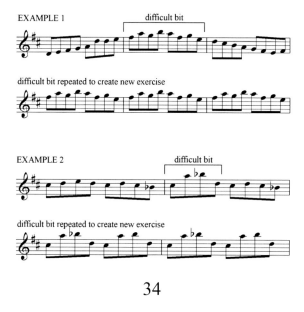

34

The word "practice" can be interpreted in a negative way, perhaps conjuring up images of being locked in a room for endless hours against your will, chained to your instrument/music stand. On the other hand, thinking of it as "focussed playing" is more positive. *Focussed* because it is a time to look more closely at what you can and can't do. *Playing* because you are playing music, even when you practice – the element of enjoyment should not be forgotten.

The best musicians are those that enjoy, even relish playing whether focussed on practice or performing.

Aim to introduce at least one new variation to a tune each time you practice. This could be a change of bowing or an alteration in the melody. See the examples below:

36

Practice time is a valuable opportunity to play music you are working on at a slower tempo. By doing this, you are able to see your playing through a magnifying glass.

Know your fiddle. Here's a picture showing all the different parts:

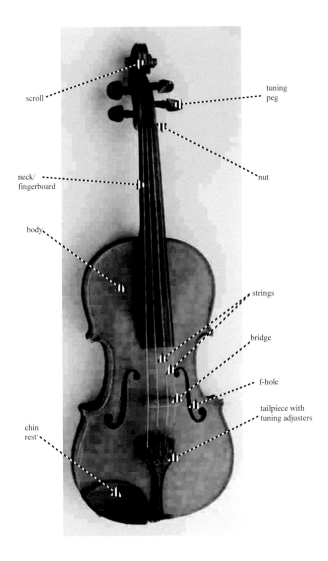

scroll

tuning peg

nut

neck/ fingerboard

body

strings

bridge

f-hole

chin rest

tailpiece with tuning adjusters

Always loosen the bow hair when not playing. When tightened, the bow hair should be taught, with the stick still obviously curved towards the hair. When loosened, the hair should be slack enough to be in contact with the stick.

39

It is not uncommon for grooves to appear on the fingerboard, in line with the strings. This is a normal sign of wear and will require attention from a repairer. This type of wear happens more frequently if the player tends to apply too much pressure when fingering the strings. It will also be a problem with fingerboards that are not made from ebony, as with cheaper instruments.

40

Every now and then it is worth having your instrument serviced by a specialist repairer. Parts of the fiddle such as the bridge, tuning pegs, fingerboard and nut will all show signs of wear in time. The sound-post (the small piece of dowel wedged inside the body of the instrument, almost under the bridge), may also need adjusting – if your fiddle sounds different, possibly after a knock, this could be because the sound-post has become dislodged.

41

If your bow doesn't have enough rosin on it, the hair will just skid over the strings without making much of a sound. If, however, you are putting lots of rosin on the bow and it's still sounding thin, this could be because your bow needs rehairing.

42

Fine-tuning adjusters (small tunings knobs that are fitted to the tailpiece) are a very useful aid to tuning. Every so often, though, it is a good idea to loosen the strings as far as the fine-tuners will allow and then tune up again using the wooden tuning pegs.

43

If you look down the neck of the fiddle, in the direction of the body, you will notice that the top of the bridge (on which the strings lie) is curved. Because of the amount of string-crossing and double-stopping that is required in traditional fiddle playing, many fiddlers prefer a less curved, flatter bridge. Ask a repairer who is conversant with traditional music.

44

If you've bought a second-hand instrument, have it checked/set up by a repairer. This also goes for an old fiddle that hasn't been used for a long time. The same can be said for the bow.

45

Keep your strings clean. A quick wipe along their length with a clean cloth after playing will lengthen their life and keep them sounding sharp for longer.

46

If a violin string wears out – sometimes the thin metal that is wound around the length of the string will start to come away – it is a sign that you should buy a new set. Don't just replace the worn out one. The other old ones will soon wear out themselves. Also, a new string will stick out like a sore thumb among older strings.

47

If you take your fiddle on an aeroplane, take it as hand luggage. If this is not possible, be aware that the strings must be loosened as the pressurised atmosphere in the hold of a plane will increase the string tension. If the strings are not loosened first, this could lead to serious damage.

If you play traditional styles on the fiddle and learn your tunes from written music, then beware. Over reliance on the printed music can make your music seem lifeless. Always be open to experimentation and variation within the basic structure of the tune.

49

If you learn a traditional/popular tune from written music, then put away the sheet music/books as soon as you have committed the tune to memory. That way, the tune is more likely to become a part of you.

50

Try transposing tunes you know well to different keys to get a fresh perspective on them. For example, look at the examples below. Notice how different the two versions of each example feel and sound:

Learn the names of the notes on the fiddle. Below is a diagram of all notes in first position.

Notice that each finger has a lower and higher position - **LP** and **HP** respectively.

The higher position for the 3rd finger is the same as the lower position for the 4th finger. As a general rule, the third finger will be used in this case if the note is sharp ($\sharp$), and the 4th finger will be used if it is flat ($\flat$). For more on sharps and flats see tip 56.

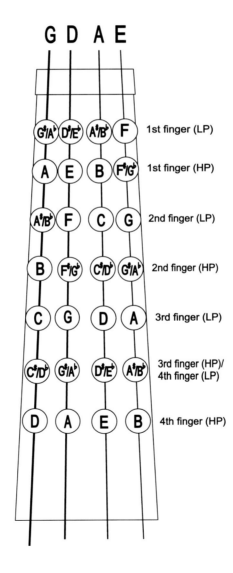

It is not vital to be able to read music in order to play traditional music. However, it can be extremely useful if you are quite new to a particular style. For someone who has grown up with traditional music around them, it will be easier to pick up the instrument as the sound will already be a part of them. Once you are more familiar with the music, though, start trying to work out tunes by ear.

Remember that written music is only half the story (if that) when it comes to performing music.

53

The distance between one note and the next note with the same name is an **octave**. For example, the distance between G on the D string, and G on the E string is one octave – the former being one octave lower than the latter. A on the E string is one octave higher than A on the A string. G on the G string is two octaves lower than G on the E string.

54

Playing every note over a single octave will give you a **chromatic scale**. Start and finish on E and you will have the E chromatic scale, start and finish on B♭ (B flat) and you will have the B♭ chromatic scale.

55

Do not confuse slurs and ties in music notation. A **slur** connects two or more notes of different pitch that are played in the same bow movement. A **tie** connects two notes of the same pitch to create one longer note. See below:

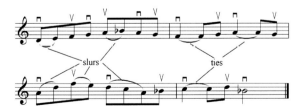

Every sharp/flat note has two names. F♯ (F sharp) can also be called G♭ (G flat) – they are the same note. The reason why one name is used instead of another depends on the musical context. F♯ is said to be the enharmonic equivalent of G♭, G♯ the enharmonic equivalent of A♭, and so on. See below:

Table of enharmonic equivalents		
G♯ (G sharp)	is the same note as	A♭ (A flat)
A♯	is the same note as	B♭
C♯	is the same note as	D♭
D♯	is the same note as	E♭
F♯	is the same note as	G♭

57

The notes of the major scale are taken from the chromatic scale. The example below is taken from the D chromatic scale. The more commonly encountered note names are used, rather than giving all enharmonic equivalents:

Chromatic scale	D Major Scale	
D	D	
E♭		T
E	E	
F		T
F♯	F♯	
G	G	S
G♯		T
A	A	
B♭		T
B	B	
C		T
C♯	C♯	
D	D	S

Some notes in the major scale have a gap of two notes, some just one. A gap of two notes is known, musically as a **tone (T)**, a gap of one is known as a **semitone (S)**.

The major scale is worked out using the formula below (T=Tone, S=Semitone):

T - T - S - T - T - T - S

Use this formula and you will arrive at the major scale for whichever note you start on:

For example, start on E flat (E♭) – apply the formula – get the E flat major scale

E♭ – F – G – A♭ – B♭ – C – D - E♭

Start on G – apply the formula – get the G major scale

G – A – B – C – D – E – F♯ - G

See tip 63 for information on which scales have sharps or flats.

The formula for the natural minor scale is:

T - S - T - T - S - T - T

Use this formula and you will arrive at the natural minor scale for the note you started on:

Start on C – apply the formula – get the C natural minor scale

C – D – E♭ – F – G – A♭ – B♭ - C

Start on B – apply the formula – get the B natural minor scale

B – C♯ - D – E – F♯ - G – A - B

See tip 63 for information on which scales have sharps or flats.

The basic blues scale is made up of five notes (it is also known as the pentatonic scale). The formula for working out a blues scale is

$$(T+S) - T - T - (T+S) - T$$

Use this formula and you will arrive at the blues scale for the note you started on.

$$E - G - A - B - D - E$$
$$A - C - D - E - G - A$$

61

Here are some more formulas to try out:

$T - S - T - T - T - S - T$	Dorian mode*
$S - T - T - T - S - T - T$	Phrygian mode
$T - T - T - S - T - T - S$	Lydian mode
$T - T - S - T - T - S - T$	Mixolydian mode

For example, start with E and apply the formula for the Dorian mode, and you will arrive at the E dorian scale. Start with B♭ and apply the formula for the Mixolydian mode and you will arrive at the B♭ mixolyian scale.

* A **mode** is a type of scale. The major and natural minor scales are also known as Ionian and Aeolian modes, respectively.

62

Here are some other, less used, enharmonic equivalents that may be encountered:

E♯	is the same note as	F
F♭	is the same note as	E
B♯	is the same note as	C
C♭	is the same note as	B

Below is a table showing which keys have sharps or flats, and how many they have. Neither C nor A minor (Am) have any sharps or flats, but both A and F sharp minor (F♯m) have 3 sharps, for example. Because G and Em have the same key signature (number of sharps or flats), they are related. G is the relative major of Em, and Em is the relative minor of G.

Key	Number of sharps or flats in key				
C/Am	No sharps or flats				
G/Em	F♯				
D/Bm	F♯	C♯			
A/F♯m	F♯	C♯	G♯		
E/C♯m	F♯	C♯	G♯	D♯	
F/Dm	B♭				
B♭/Gm	B♭	E♭			
E♭/Cm	B♭	E♭	A♭		
A♭/Fm	B♭	E♭	A♭	D♭	

64

Traditional music has always been learned best by ear. To learn a traditional style successfully, it is vital to listen to as much as possible, whether this is through playing with friends, going to gigs or listening to recordings.

65

Traditional tunes tend to stick in the memory better if learned by ear, rather than from written music.

66

Don't rely too much on tune names – there are countless instances of tunes sharing the same name or a single tune having several names.

67

Unusual time-signatures, such as 7/8 and 11/8, can be easier to understand if broken up into smaller chunks. For example 7/8 (7 eighth-beats) could be split into 4+3 eighth-beats and counted as:

1, 2, 3, 4, 1, 2, 3
1, 2, 3, 4, 1, 2, 3
1, 2, 3, 4, 1, 2, 3

(the first beat shown in bold)
Alternatively the bar could be split up as 3+4 and counted as follows:

1, 2, 3, 1, 2, 3, 4
1, 2, 3, 1, 2, 3, 4
1, 2, 3, 1, 2, 3, 4

11/8 would be split into 4+3+4:

1, 2, 3, 4, 1, 2, 3, 1, 2, 3, 4
1, 2, 3, 4, 1, 2, 3, 1, 2, 3, 4
1, 2, 3, 4, 1, 2, 3, 1, 2, 3, 4

There is no *physical* difference between the fiddle and violin. The only difference is in the way they are played. If a classical player picked up the instrument he would be more likely to call it a violin. He may then pass it to a traditional player (if it wasn't too expensive!) who would probably call it a fiddle. They would both be right.

69

If you find that you are stuck in a rut with 6/8 tunes, always playing the first beat of each bar with a down-bow, try reversing the bowing for a whole tune as an exercise..

Look at the examples below for further clarification:

Example 2 has the same music as example 1, with the bowing reversed.

A good traditional player will be able to swap freely between these bowing patterns within a 6/8 tune, as in example 3.

It can be very effective in 6/8 tunes to shift the emphasis from the usual 1ˢᵗ and 4ᵗʰ beats of the bar…

…to the 3ʳᵈ and 6ᵗʰ beats:

This shouldn't be overdone, though – the occasional shift of emphasis is far more effective.

71

When learning a traditional style of music, it is always better to try and copy the sound you hear. If using written music, remember that it is just a guide. The subtleties of the style will be easier to pick up by ear. Think how a child learns to speak its native language – through listening and copying. Reading comes later. The process of learning to play traditional music is very similar.

72

A great feature of traditional fiddle playing is the double-stop. This involves playing more than one string at once. There are three different sorts:

i)   Playing two open strings simultaneously
ii)   Playing one open and one fingered note.
iii)   Playing two fingered notes.

A potential difficulty with ii) and iii) is that of left hand fingers getting in the way of strings they shouldn't be playing. See tips 20 and 21 for advice on this.

73

If learning a tune from a collection, bear in mind that the tune you are looking at is only one player's version of the tune. It is not the "right" version of the tune – no such thing exists with traditional music. So use the written music as a guide, pick up ideas from it (as well as from other sources), and develop your own version of the tune.

74

Ornaments and embellishments such as grace notes, cuts, rolls and triplets play an important role, especially in traditional music. They are, however of secondary importance to the tune. They serve to decorate. In the same way, an ornament on the mantelpiece is not part of the structure of the room - it is an addition that should enhance the surroundings. If the room is in a state, or maybe even half-built, then the ornament will serve no purpose.

75

Sometimes it may be difficult to accommodate intricate ornamentation within a tune that is played at speed. Never allow this to detract from the tune, by hindering its flow. Rather leave out the ornaments.

76

Great fiddle players are also likely to be natural improvisers.

The selection of tunes that they know will change and grow organically, unlike a static repertoire of "pieces". The tunes will change over time, as the player's style develops and matures.

Take steps to achieve this by not sticking slavishly to a particular version of a tune. Allow variations to appear in your playing.

77

Set aside some time in practice sessions to just experiment. Feel free to make discordant, ugly sounds in your search for something beautiful or interesting.

Experimentation is the foundation of the exciting world of improvisation and composition.

78

Improvisation is not a skill that just a small, gifted minority are born with. It takes work and lots of patience.

First attempts in improvisation are bound to seem unsure and lacking in confidence, just as first attempts at playing the trumpet, driving a car or baking bread will.

Practicing this skill will result in a more assured sound.

79

Once you have spent some time improvising, have come up with some good ideas and can write them down, you have moved into the realms of composition. Everyone is capable of creating and, if you can play an instrument, then you are capable of composing.

Many are daunted by the word "composer", however. The word conjures up pictures of untouchable geniuses such as Beethoven and Mozart. Remember, though, that one does not have to be Beethoven in order to compose.

If a run of notes works particularly well in a solo, do not be afraid to repeat it straight away, or draw on it later on in your solo.

Repetition is a vital ingredient in improvisation. A solo without repeated material will seem to wander aimlessly.

81

If improvising a solo, remember that pauses say as much as fast runs of notes. A balance of fast notes, slow notes and pauses will make for a more interesting solo.

82

If improvising a solo within a song, there are two possible approaches:

- Use the key of the song as a starting point. For example, if the song is in D major, start by exploring the D major scale. If the song has a bluesy feel and is in E, start by exploring the E blues scale (*see tips 58-60*). Look out for key changes in the song. A chorus can often be in a different key to the verses.

- Use the melody of the song as a starting point. Play the main melody of the song and add extra notes/ornaments to it from the chosen scale.

Using elements of the song melody along with other ideas taken from the scale will make for an interesting, balanced solo.

83

Notes outside the scale of a song or accompaniment can also be very effective if used sparingly in a solo. These sort of notes need to sound like they were intended, rather than accidental.

84

If a discordant note is hit when performing a solo, don't think of it as a mistake. Instead, use it as an opportunity to resolve the note up or down to a note that does work.

85

Many solos use the *question and answer* technique, or *statement and reply*. Think of a run of notes as a short phrase or statement, and the next run of notes as a reply.

Do this a few times and you will have a dialogue or conversation. The statements and replies can be long or short, said quickly or meditatively

86

If you have neighbours or family members that don't share your love of fiddle music, it may be necessary to buy a mute!

There are a variety available, all of which attach to the bridge. Metal mutes, in the form of a weight that fits on top of the bridge, cut the sound down to a whisper, while wooden and rubber mutes will let more sound out, retaining some tone as a result.

87

Electronic tuners are very useful for tuning up in a noisy environment. However, it is better not to rely too heavily on these devices and to trust your ear instead.

88

Accuracy and comfort can be greatly improved by using a shoulder rest. If one isn't used, the instrument is not supported properly between the chin and collar bone.

This means that the left hand has to be burdened with supporting the fiddle, cutting down on its freedom of movement.

While this is not such a problem for the traditional player who rarely moves out of first position, it seems unnecessary to give this extra job to the left hand when all is needed is a shoulder rest, or other form of padding.

89

If you use an electronic tuner, tune up your instrument and play the pairs of adjacent strings together (G+D, D+A, A+E), listening carefully.

Get your ear used to what the notes sound like when perfectly in tune. This is particularly useful when learning.

90

Trying out different makes of string is a very expensive business. It may be helpful to know that synthetic strings give a mellower, softer tone and steel give a louder more strident one. Synthetic strings are also known for their quick responsiveness – something that suits the rapid playing associated with traditional music.

91

String cleaner and instrument cleaner are useful for removing the inevitable build up of dust, rosin and other matter. While many traditional players like to leave a layer of rosin dust on the fiddle, near the bridge, it is unlikely that this will positively affect the sound of the instrument. It would be more useful as a store of recycled rosin to be used when you run out!

92

Make sure your gig bag contains clothes pegs. They are invaluable for holding music/set lists down on a stand when playing out doors! There's nothing more embarrassing, when gigging, to have to halt your playing to chase a piece of paper in front of everyone. While you're at it, put some mosquito repellent in there, too. When playing outdoors, you are powerless against these dreaded creatures.

93

Other than an electric tuner, the most accurate and reliable pitch source is given by the tuning fork. These are inexpensive and fit easily into a fiddle case or pocket. Pitch pipes are not a great idea, as they tend to go out of tune themselves, which rather defeats their purpose!

94

If possible, take a spare bow out when performing. Bow hair is held in place by a tiny wedge in the tip, and it is not unknown for these to come loose, flying across the room never to be seen again. You are then left to play pizzicato for the rest of the evening.

95

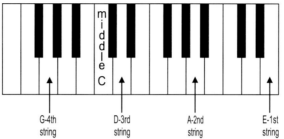

G-4th string   D-3rd string   A-2nd string   E-1st string

If using a keyboard or piano to tune up, use the notes shown above to give you correct pitches for the fiddle strings. Middle C is the C note found in the middle of the keyboard.

96

When performing in front of an audience, keep in mind that you are your own most scathing critic. Nobody else listens to your playing as critically as you do. Most people are impressed by the fact that you are able to get up and play in front of people at all!

97

Playing with other musicians is a great way to really move forward with any instrument, although it is very important to keep an ear on what others are playing. Disappearing too far into your own world will weaken the sound of the group.

In the absence of other musicians, play along with recordings of your favourite fiddle players and bands.

98

It is possible to learn a great deal by recording yourself and listening back to your playing. You may well find out some interesting things you never knew about your playing, both bad and good!

Think of embellishments or ornamentation in your playing as herbs and spices being added to a dish. A little brings out the flavour of the ingredients, while heavy-handedness will overpower them and spoil the dish.

100

It is easier to tune *up* an out-of-tune string. That is, when it is lower than the desired pitch. If a string is out of tune, make it lower (even if it is higher) and then tune it up.

101

Other musicians can be a great source of new ideas, advice and criticism. Always take advice graciously, and make your own informed opinion from the various sources you have around you, whether they be other musicians, teachers, recordings or books.

WWW.MELBAY.COM